Parts of Plants

Roots

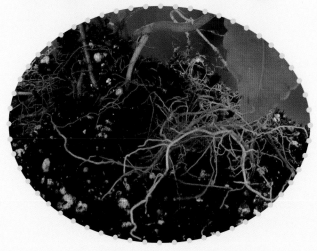

Vijaya Khisty Bodach

raintree

a Capstone company — publishers for children

Raintree is an imprint of Capstone Global Library Limited, a company incorporated in England and Wales
having its registered office at 264 Banbury Road, Oxford, OX2 7DY – Registered company number: 6695582

www.raintree.co.uk
myorders@raintree.co.uk

Text © Capstone Global Library Limited 2017
The moral rights of the proprietor have been asserted.

Edited by Sarah L Schuette
Designed by Jennifer Bergstrom
Picture research by Kelly Garvin
Originated by Capstone Global Library Ltd
Printed and bound in China.

ISBN 978 1 4747 3551 3
20 19 18 17 16
10 9 8 7 6 5 4 3 2 1

British Library Cataloguing in Publication Data
A full catalogue record for this book is available from the British Library.

Acknowledgements
We would like to thank the following for permission to reproduce photographs:
Capstone Studio: Karon Dubke, cover, 1; Shutterstock: Adrian T Jones, 11, Bernhard Richter, 21, David Kay,
19, fotografos, 15, Hayati Kayhan, 17, Jim Parkin, 13, Lubava, top 22, bottom 22, Maks Narodenko, right 22,
Nikishina E, 5, showcake, 7, Smit, 9

We would like to thank Judson R Scott, past President of American Society of Consulting Arborists for his
invaluable help in the preparation of this book.

Every effort has been made to contact copyright holders of material reproduced in this book. Any omissions
will be rectified in subsequent printings if notice is given to the publisher.

All the Internet addresses (URLs) given in this book were valid at the time of going to press. However, due to
the dynamic nature of the Internet, some addresses may have changed, or sites may have changed or ceased
to exist since publication. While the author and publisher regret any inconvenience this may cause readers, no
responsibility for any such changes can be accepted by either the author or the publisher.

Contents

Plants need roots

Roots keep plants
from falling over.
Roots grow down
into the ground.

Roots get food

for the whole plant.

They suck up food

and water from the soil.

Roots send food

up plant stems.

Stems carry the food

to the rest of the plant.

9

All kinds of roots

Long tree roots spread out
under the soil.

They search for water below.

Shallow cactus roots
soak up rain quickly.
They store water
for the plant.

Water lily roots

grow down into the mud.

Roots keep the plants

from floating away.

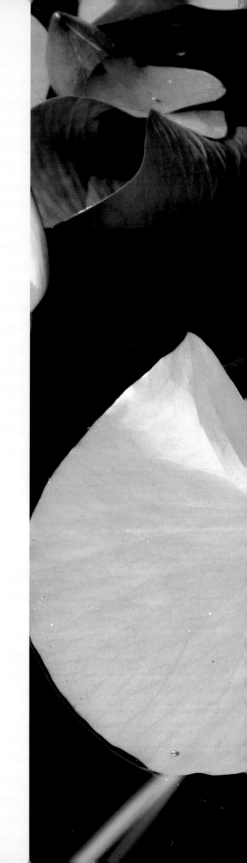

Roots we eat

We eat some roots.

Carrots are the tap roots
of green leafy carrot plants.

Turnips are root vegetables.

They taste good in soups

and salads.

Wonderful roots

Deep or shallow,
thick or thin,
roots help plants
stay alive.

Parts of a sweetcorn plant

seed

stem

roots

leaves

Glossary

soil   earth where plants grow; most plants get their food and water from the soil

stem   long main part of a plant that makes leaves; food gathered by roots moves through the stem to the rest of the plant

tap root   long, thick plant part that grows into the ground; carrots are tap roots

Find out more

All About Roots (All About Plants), Claire Throp (Raintree, 2015)

Plants (Real Size Science), Rebecca Rissman (Raintree, 2014)

Roots, Stems, Leaves and Flowers: All About Plant Parts (Fundamental Science Key Stage 1), Ruth Owen (Ruby Tuesday Books, 2016)

Index

Websites

http://www.firstschoolyears.com/science/living/interactive/growing-plants.swf
Learn about the parts and life cycle of plants with these fun, interactive activities.

http://www.dkfindout.com/us/animals-and-nature/plants/parts-plant/
Find out all about the different parts of a plant.